The Cat and the Dancing Hat

Best Wishes
Linda Jones
& Carole M.
x

The Cat and the Dancing Hat
First published in the UK 2024 ©

Author – Linda Jones
Illustration and book cover – Carole Marsh

Publisher – Bavoom Publishing

ISBN 978-1-0687301-5-3

httlnps://lindajonesukauthor.com

For Phoebe, Evelyn and Max

In my back garden was a
large oak tree,
with a green painted
fence that was taller
than me.

Mr Hodges, next door, grew
vegetables and flowers.
My mum kept trying
but somehow, they kept dying.
She blamed our cat...

Marmalade, you see, was
not a nice creature.
She dug up our borders,
messed with the water feature,
then scrambled through Mum's fragile
sweet peas.
My mum was mad!
Mostly with my dad,
because he laughed and said
he wanted a dog!

Sometimes at night that naughty cat
would spring
up onto the fence and begin to sing.

Yowling and wailing at the top of
her voice!
Dad thought there was a tiger
lurking inside her...

or a werewolf perhaps?

Marmalade chased birds,
butterflies and frogs.
Leapt through my mum's
seedlings,
to wind up next door's dogs.

They went crazy,
yelping and howling,
while she licked her coat...

and coughed up fur balls!

Afraid of nothing,
she was the queen of our road.
Not even rats
or the huge green-backed toad
scared her.

Or at least, not until one day...

Out of nowhere, a big, red hat
appeared.
It moved, as if by magic, which was
really weird!
Twitching and jiggling it twirled
around,
then, without making a sound,
it headed towards our path...

From behind came a *Grroowl*
and a thump...
Marmalade appeared.
She was on the hunt!
Ears flat to her head, she stalked
the hat.
Claws reaching out, she gave it
a crafty bat...

Zoom - it sped away, as if
enchanted!

Grroowl
Zoom

Across the grass,
it darted past
the sunflowers and sweet peas.
Marmalade went crazy,
as it dashed under daisies
that fluttered in the breeze.

Up and down,
round and around,
the hat was swift and so clever!
Rushing left,
swirling right,
the chase seemed to last forever...

Marmalade wasn't giving up - she
pounced!
The hat turned over, and out
bounced...
one very angry grey squirrel!

Meeoow! Cried Marmalade,
as the squirrel's teeth nipped her nose.
Where that squirrel went, I really
don't know!

Meeeoow!

But our cat was sulking at the top
of the tree...

Me - I kept that hat,
hoping Marmalade would think I was
the squirrel!

In Grandma's House

Another book in the Marmalade Orange series
from award-winning author Linda Jones.
Delightfully illustrated by Carole Marsh.
A rhyming tale about a mischievous cat.

Marmalade Orange,
eyes piercingly blue,
a tail that swished,
sometimes she hissed loudly too...

Marmalade Orange always manages to find trouble
and when a mouse escapes from right under her nose,
Marmalade is in hot pursuit...
Can she catch the little creature
or will that clever mouse win the day?

In Grandma's House

By Linda Jones
& Carole Marsh

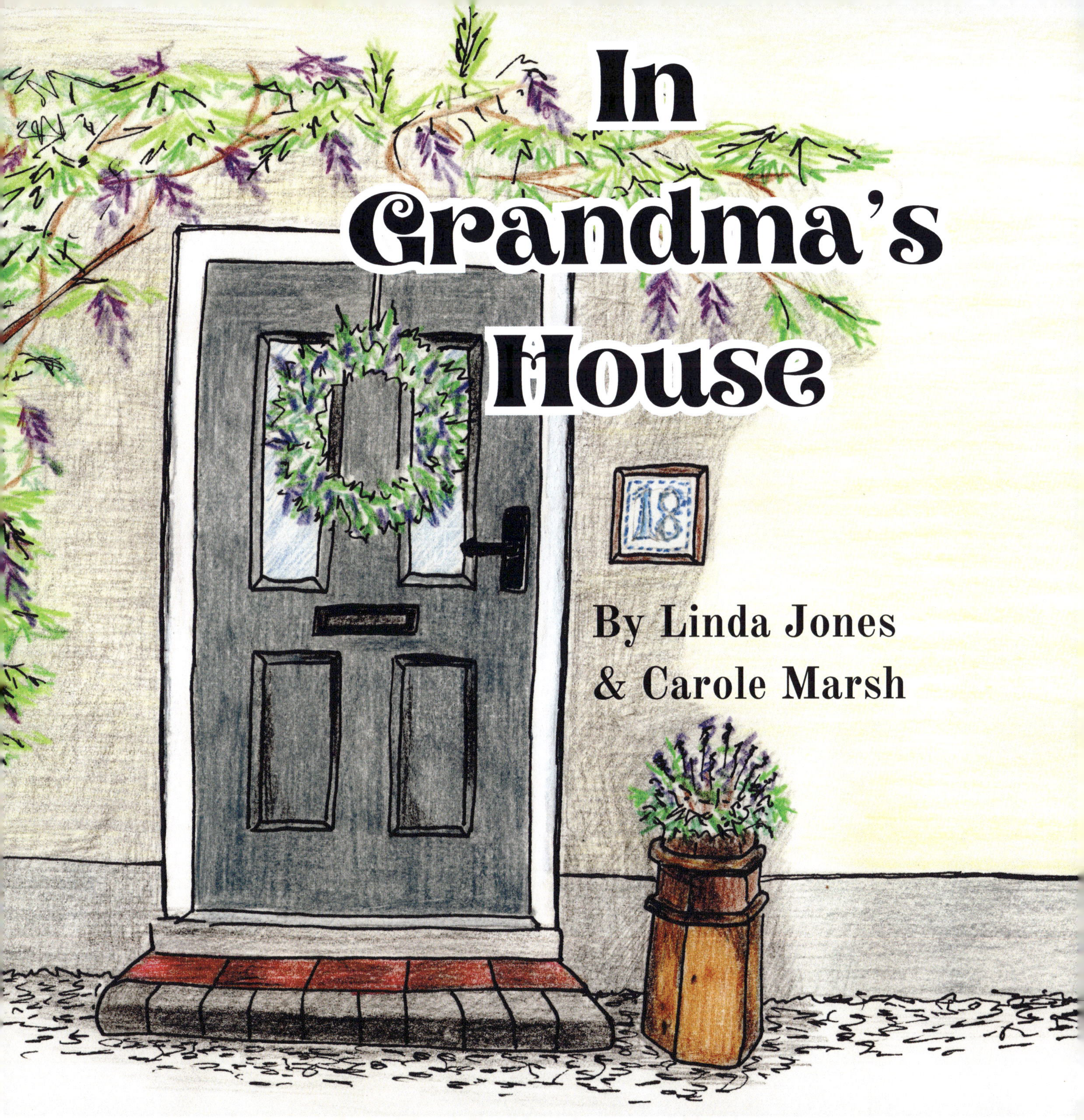

Printed in Great Britain
by Amazon

48167321R00021